TODAY'S 12 HOTTEST
TV SUPERSTARS

by Annabelle Tometich

www.12StoryLibrary.com

Copyright © 2015 by Peterson Publishing Company, North Mankato, MN 56003. All rights reserved. No part of this book may be reproduced or utilized in any form or by any means without written permission from the publisher.

12-Story Library is an imprint of Peterson Publishing Company and Press Room Editions.

Produced for 12-Story Library by Red Line Editorial

Photographs ©: AP Images, cover, 1; Helga Esteb/Shutterstock Images, 5, 6, 10, 15, 19, 22, 24, 28, 29; Kristopher Long/Comedy Central/AP Images, 7; Shutterstock Images, 8, 16, 17, 18, 20, 26; Rex Features/AP Images, 9; Christian Bertrand/Shutterstock Images, 11; Douglas Gorenstein/NBC/AP Images, 13; Jaguar PS/Shutterstock Images, 21, 25; Ron Tom/ABC/AP Images, 27

ISBN
978-1-63235-023-7 (hardcover)
978-1-63235-083-1 (paperback)
978-1-62143-064-3 (hosted ebook)

Library of Congress Control Number: 2014946814

Printed in the United States of America
Mankato, MN
October, 2014

Go beyond the book. Get free, up-to-date content on this topic at 12StoryLibrary.com.

TABLE OF CONTENTS

TY BURRELL IS TV'S FUNNY DAD

In 2014, Ty Burrell earned more than $175,000 per episode of *Modern Family*. That's not bad for a guy who once lived in a van. Burrell grew up in Oregon. His dad was a family therapist. His mom stayed at home to raise Ty and his older brother, Duncan. The boys were always being silly. They had competitions to see who could make their dad laugh first.

During a high school talent show, Burrell learned he loved the stage. He wasn't a very good student, though. He failed out of college. When Burrell was 19, his father died of cancer. It pushed him to go back to school. He studied theater and learned how plays are produced. Burrell started taking acting seriously.

Burrell starred in small college plays. He didn't earn much money from these roles. To make ends meet, he lived in his van. In the meantime, he kept working hard for bigger roles.

5

Number of Screen Actors Guild Awards Burrell has earned for his role in *Modern Family*.

Full Name: Tyler Gerald Burrell

Birth Date: August 22, 1967

Birthplace: Grants Pass, Oregon

Breakthrough Moment: Role of Phil Dunphy on the hit TV show *Modern Family*

Awards: 5 Screen Actors Guild Awards, 2 Emmy Awards for *Modern Family*

Burrell and Julie Bowen, who plays Phil's wife on *Modern Family*, pose with their Emmy Awards in 2011.

In 2001, he earned a small part in the movie *Black Hawk Down*. In 2004, he landed another role in the movie *Dawn of the Dead*.

In 2009, Burrell was chosen to play Phil Dunphy on *Modern Family*. Phil Dunphy's character is a dad who tries hard to be cool. Phil Dunphy is awkward and funny. Burrell's character makes people laugh each week. This role won Burrell an Emmy for Outstanding Supporting Actor in a Comedy Series in 2014.

STEPHEN COLBERT TAKES OVER FOR LETTERMAN

Stephen Colbert is the youngest of 11 children. He was born in Washington, DC, but grew up in Charleston, South Carolina. In high school, Colbert acted in plays. He went to college at Northwestern University near Chicago, Illinois, where he studied theater.

After college, Colbert worked with a comedy troupe in Chicago. With this group, he worked on improvisation, the art of acting on the spot without practice or a script. Then he started writing jokes for TV shows. Colbert is known for his satire. Satire is when someone uses comedy and jokes to expose problems. Using satire, Colbert jokes about and exposes problems in the media and government.

In 1997, *The Daily Show* hired Colbert to play a fake news reporter. *The Daily Show* pokes fun at traditional news programs. The fake newsman shared Colbert's name. Audiences loved the character. In 2005, his character got his own show. It was called *The Colbert Report*. In April 2014, Colbert landed his biggest role yet. He was selected to take over David Letterman's spot on CBS's *Late Show* in 2015.

Colbert stands with his awards at the Emmys in 2013.

Colbert with guests Jon Stewart (right) and Trevor Potter on *The Colbert Report* in 2012

7

Number of Emmy Awards Colbert has earned throughout his career.

Full Name: Stephen Tyrone Colbert

Birth Date: May 13, 1964

Birthplace: Washington, DC

Breakthrough Moment: 1997 appearance on *The Daily Show*, a nightly comedy-news show

Awards: 7 Emmy Awards for his work on *The Daily Show* and *The Colbert Report*

STEPHEN'S SATIRE

It can be hard to take Colbert seriously. That's the thing about satire. On *The Colbert Report* he plays a stubborn TV anchor. His character can only see things his way. Colbert has interviewed presidents and other celebrities. Colbert interviews them in character. On the show, he makes fun of news anchors who take themselves too seriously.

ELLEN DeGENERES RULES DAYTIME TV

Ellen DeGeneres grew up in Louisiana with a love of animals and comedy. Her brother Vance became an actor and comedian. But it was Ellen who would make the family name famous.

DeGeneres received her star on the Hollywood Walk of Fame in 2012.

8

DeGeneres started performing stand-up comedy when she was 23. By 1986, she was telling jokes on *The Tonight Show Starring Johnny Carson*. Carson, the show's host, liked her. He invited her onto the show for an interview. She was the first female comedian he ever asked to interview.

In the 1990s, she played the lead role in the sitcom *Ellen*. In 1997, like herself in real life, DeGeneres's character on the show came out as gay. She was the first gay lead character in prime time TV history.

DeGeneres started her talk show, *The Ellen DeGeneres Show*, in 2003. And the show is still going strong. It has produced more than 1,000 episodes. DeGeneres begins each one by telling jokes and dancing with her audience. She uses humor to make her guests feel comfortable. The show has been so popular that it has won 48 Emmy Awards since 2004.

Since the show's beginning, DeGeneres has starred in the movie *Finding Nemo* as the voice of Dory. She will also star in the 2015 sequel titled *Finding Dory*. She has hosted two Oscars awards shows and has been a judge on *American Idol*.

23
Age at which DeGeneres began stand-up comedy.

Full Name: Ellen Lee DeGeneres

Birth Date: January 26, 1958

Birthplace: Metairie, Louisiana

Breakthrough Moment: DeGeneres's sitcom, *Ellen,* debuted in 1994.

Awards: *The Ellen DeGeneres Show* has won 48 Emmy Awards since 2004.

DeGeneres gets the audience and guest stars, even First Lady Michelle Obama, to dance with her on *The Ellen DeGeneres Show.*

ZOOEY DESCHANEL AS THE *NEW GIRL*

Zooey Deschanel grew up in the entertainment business. Her father was a cinematographer. Her mom was an actress. Zooey's older sister, Emily, stars in the hit TV series *Bones*. As a child, Deschanel traveled with her father to shoot movies. She visited many countries around the world.

Deschanel attended Crossroads School for Arts and Sciences, a performing arts high school in Santa Monica, California. She loved singing and acting. She hoped to star in musicals on Broadway. In 1998, Deschanel got her first acting job. She landed a small part on the TV show *Veronica's Closet*. In 2003, she sang and acted alongside Will Ferrell in the movie *Elf*. And in 2011, Deschanel's sitcom *New Girl* debuted.

Deschanel with other cast members of *New Girl* in 2013

2009

Year Fallon transitioned from *SNL* star to *Late Night* host.

Full Name: James Thomas Fallon Jr.

Birth Date: September 19, 1974

Birthplace: Brooklyn, New York

Breakthrough Moment: Joined the cast of *Saturday Night Live* in 1998

Awards: 2 Emmy Awards, 1 Grammy Award

himself too seriously. He's famous for cracking up during sketches. He usually makes his audience crack up too.

6

MINDY KALING'S OWN PROJECT

Mindy Kaling's parents moved to the United States from India. Her mother was a doctor. Her dad worked as an architect. As a child, Mindy was obsessed with comedy shows. She watched *Saturday Night Live* over and over. She memorized the jokes. She even learned the names of the producers.

When it came time for college, Kaling studied playwriting. She joined the school's improv troupe and wrote comic strips for the school paper. After college, Kaling started performing stand-up comedy. She also starred in a friend's play. In the play, Kaling played the role of movie star Ben Affleck. She looked nothing like him. But she was funny.

A producer of the TV comedy *The Office* saw her in the play. He was impressed with her. He hired her to write for *The Office*. She also starred in the show. Kaling played the part of Kelly Kapoor.

100 MOST INFLUENTIAL PEOPLE

In 2013, *Time* magazine honored Kaling by naming her one of the 100 most influential people in the world. It called Kaling "brilliant, wonderful, and hilarious." It said, "To be made fun of by Mindy is to feel special."

In 2012, Kaling got her own show. It is called *The Mindy Project.* She plays a doctor in the show. She modeled the character after her own mother. In its first season, the show won a Critics Choice Award for Most Exciting New Series.

2013
Year Kaling was named one of the 100 most influential people by *Time* magazine.

Full Name: Vera Mindy Chokalingam

Birth Date: June 24, 1979

Birthplace: Cambridge, Massachusetts

Breakthrough Moment: Kaling starred as Kelly Kapoor on *The Office* from 2005 to 2013.

Awards: 2 Screen Actors Guild Awards, 3 Emmy nominations

In 2012, Kaling began starring in *The Mindy Project,* which airs on FOX.

JIM PARSONS SHOWS NERDS CAN BE COOL

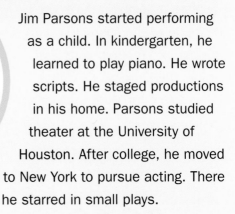

Parsons plays an awkward yet funny genius on *The Big Bang Theory*.

Jim Parsons started performing as a child. In kindergarten, he learned to play piano. He wrote scripts. He staged productions in his home. Parsons studied theater at the University of Houston. After college, he moved to New York to pursue acting. There he starred in small plays.

Parsons landed a recurring role in the TV show *Judging Amy*. He also played a small part in the 2004 film *Garden State.* Parsons's big break came in 2006. He auditioned for the part of Sheldon Cooper on the TV comedy *The Big Bang Theory*. Parsons's performance blew the show's producer away. Parsons was hired to play the nerdy scientist Sheldon Cooper. While Parsons's character is a genius, he is awkward around others. This makes his interactions with other characters on the show hilarious to watch. The show became a huge hit. In 2014, *The Big Bang Theory* was

Parsons and *The Big Bang Theory* cast share their People's Choice Award in 2010.

$1 million

Amount of money Parsons will receive for each episode of *The Big Bang Theory*, beginning with season eight.

Full Name: James Joseph Parsons

Birth Date: March 24, 1973

Birthplace: Houston, Texas

Breakthrough Moment: In 2007, Parsons first appeared as Sheldon Cooper on *The Big Bang Theory*.

Awards: 3 Emmy Awards, 1 Golden Globe Award

the No. 1 show on TV. It averaged 20 million viewers per episode.

Parsons is one of the highest paid actors on TV. In 2014, he signed on to receive $1 million per episode, starting with the eighth season of *The Big Bang Theory*.

AMY POEHLER WEARS MANY HATS

Amy Poehler grew up near Boston, Massachusetts. She starred in school plays as a child. In college, she joined an improv troupe. The troupe was called My Mother's Fleabag. Poehler graduated from college in 1993. She then moved to Chicago. She joined a famous improv company there.

Poehler met Tina Fey while doing improv. The two became close friends when they both starred in *Saturday Night Live*. On the show, Poehler played a range of characters. She even poked fun at her hometown of Boston. Poehler hosted *SNL*'s *Weekend Update* segment with Fey. Poehler starred on *SNL* from 2001 to 2008. Between that time, she and Fey also starred in two movies together. These two movies, *Mean Girls* in 2004 and *Baby Mama* in 2008, were both comedies.

Poehler (right) and Tina Fey pose together at the 2012 Golden Globes after party.

100TH EPISODE

Parks and Recreation

Poehler celebrates *Parks and Recreation*'s 100th episode in 2013.

2

Number of Golden Globe Awards Poehler has hosted.

Full Name: Amy Meredith Poehler

Birth Date: September 16, 1971

Birthplace: Newton, Massachusetts

Breakthrough Moment: In 2001, Poehler became a cast member on *Saturday Night Live*.

Awards: 1 Golden Globe Award, 10 Emmy nominations

In 2009, Poehler's sitcom *Parks and Recreation* debuted. Poehler plays the part of Leslie Knope. Knope works for the Parks Department in a small town in Indiana. She takes her job very seriously. But the people around her don't care nearly as much. The part earned Poehler a Golden Globe for Best Actress in 2014.

ANDY SAMBERG SHINES IN *SNL DIGITAL SHORTS*

Andy Samberg grew up in California. He met two of his best friends in junior high school. Andy, Jorma Taccone, and Akiva Schaffer loved to perform comedy sketches together. They did it to make their friends laugh. They joked that it was also a good way to not get bullied.

After high school, Samberg moved to New York for college. In 2000, he graduated from New York University. He earned a degree in film. After college, Samberg reunited with his friends. They formed a comedy troupe. They called it The Lonely Island.

The trio bought a video camera. They filmed short comedy sketches and posted them on the Internet. The sketches went viral. In 2005, Samberg and his friends were invited to write for the MTV Movie Awards. Jimmy Fallon was the host. He thought the guys were very funny.

Samberg with friends Taccone (left) and Schaffer (right) at a movie premiere in 2007

2014

Year Samberg won a Golden Globe Award for Best Actor.

Full Name: David Andrew Samberg

Birth Date: August 18, 1978

Birthplace: Mill Valley, California

Breakthrough Moment: In 2005, Samberg joined the cast of *Saturday Night Live*.

Awards: 1 Golden Globe Award, 1 Emmy Award

SNL DIGITAL SHORTS

Samberg became famous for his *SNL Digital Shorts*. The brief sketches included songs and raps. They featured famous stars such as Justin Timberlake. The *SNL Digital Shorts* gained millions of views. They even earned Samberg an Emmy Award.

Fallon helped them get jobs on *Saturday Night Live*.

Samberg was on *SNL* from 2005 to 2012. He convinced celebrities to do hilarious things. He had movie star Natalie Portman perform in a rap video. Samberg and rapper T. Pain rapped an entire song about being on a boat. He left *SNL* to pursue other kinds of acting. In 2013, Samberg starred in the action comedy show *Brooklyn Nine-Nine*. In 2014, the show earned two Golden Globe Awards. Samberg won one for Best Actor.

Samberg plays detective Jake Peralta in *Brooklyn Nine-Nine*.

RYAN SEACREST: VOICE OF RADIO AND FACE OF TV

Seacrest began hosting *American Idol* in 2002.

Ryan Seacrest got his start in radio. As a child, he listened to famous DJs such as Casey Kasem. He studied and copied the way they talked. In high school, Seacrest was

often teased for being overweight. The teasing motivated him to work harder. He started delivering the morning announcements at his school. In college, he worked as a radio DJ.

After college, Seacrest moved to Los Angeles, California. He wanted to pursue his radio career. He created and hosted his own afternoon radio program. But it was hosting *American Idol* that made Seacrest famous. Seacrest started hosting *American Idol* in 2002. He originally auditioned to be a judge on the show. But the producers liked his energy. They hired him as a host.

In 2005, Seacrest began hosting the entertainment show *E! News*. He also has two national radio shows and has appeared on NBC's *Today Show*. He helped cover the 2012 Olympics in London. Seacrest

2
Number of Emmy Awards Seacrest has earned.

Full Name: Ryan John Seacrest

Birth Date: December 24, 1974

Birthplace: Atlanta, Georgia

Breakthrough Moment: In 2002, Seacrest was chosen to host *American Idol.*

Awards: 2 Emmy Awards

owns production companies. He has created several reality TV shows, including *Keeping Up with the Kardashians.* Seacrest remains upbeat and energetic. He works hard to stay on top of his many projects. He works long days. He is often called the "hardest working man in showbiz."

SOFIA VERGARA: TV'S HIGHEST-PAID ACTRESS

Vergara and Ed O'Neill play a married couple on *Modern Family.*

Sofia Vergara grew up in Colombia. While she was in high school, talent agents spotted her on the beach. They asked her to star in a Pepsi commercial. She was just 17 years old. Vergara went to college in Colombia. She studied to become a dentist. But she got more offers to model and be on TV. She chose show business.

Vergara started hosting Spanish-language shows in Colombia. In 2002, she landed her first movie role in the comedy crime thriller *Big Trouble.* In 2009, Vergara began starring in the hit TV show *Modern Family.* She plays the role of Gloria Delgado-Pritchett. *Modern Family*'s creators designed the role specifically for Vergara. They knew she was the perfect person for it. The part has earned Vergara four Emmy nominations for Outstanding Supporting Actress.

Vergara with *Modern Family* costars at the Emmy Awards in 2011

Modern Family was an instant hit. In 2014, it was the No. 2 show on TV. Vergara isn't just a beauty on the show. She is also funny. In 2013, Vergara was the highest-paid actress on TV. She earned an astonishing $30 million that year.

VERGARA'S MANY TALENTS

Vergara is more than an actress. She is also a designer. Vergara designs a clothing line for Kmart and a furniture line for Rooms To Go. Vergara is also a spokeswoman for Cover Girl and Diet Pepsi.

17

Age at which Vergara appeared in her first Pepsi commercial.

Full Name: Sofia Margarita Vergara

Birth Date: July 10, 1972

Birthplace: Barranquilla, Colombia

Breakthrough Moment: In 2008, Vergara starred in the film *Meet The Browns.*

Awards: 2 Screen Actors Guild Awards, 4 Emmy nominations, 4 Golden Globe nominations

KERRY WASHINGTON: *SCANDAL'S* LEAD ROLE

Kerry Washington grew up in the Bronx neighborhood of New York City. As a child, she took ballet lessons. In high school, she joined a theater group. She earned a theater scholarship to George Washington University.

Washington transitioned from stage to film in 2000. That year she starred in the drama *Our Song*. In 2001, she landed the part of Chenille in *Save the Last Dance.* Chenille is a teen mom who befriends the main character, a ballet dancer named Sara. Chenille helps Sara develop her dance skills through hip-hop.

In 2004, Washington starred in the movie *Ray.* She played the wife of singer Ray Charles. She earned rave reviews. After years of success in movie acting, Washington moved on to TV. In 2012, she began starring

Washington can play funny roles, but she most often plays serious roles.

10.5 million

Number of viewers who tuned in to watch Washington in *Scandal's* season three debut episode.

Full Name: Kerry Marisa Washington

Birth Date: January 31, 1977

Birthplace: New York, New York

Breakthrough Moment: Washington starred in the 2001 film *Save the Last Dance.*

Awards: 1 Golden Globe nomination, 2 Emmy nominations

Washington acts with Tony Goldwyn (left) and Scott Foley on *Scandal.*

in the TV series *Scandal. Scandal* is a political drama. Washington plays the lead character Olivia Pope. She was the first black actress to play a lead role in a drama since 1974. The part has earned her several awards nominations.

FACT SHEET

- It wasn't until the 1940s that TV caught on. In 1947, several major TV shows premiered. These included classics such as *The Ed Sullivan Show*, *Howdy Doody*, and *Candid Camera*. Soon the United States had one of its first TV stars. Milton Berle hosted *Texaco Star Theater*. He sang and danced. He told jokes and made a fool of himself. People loved it. The show was a huge hit. Stores would close early in order for workers to be home in time to catch "Uncle Miltie."

- By 1951 cable had spread from coast to coast in the United States. This meant that people in California could watch the same shows as people in New York. There was a huge demand for TV shows. In 1951, the show *I Love Lucy* debuted. It starred comedian Lucille Ball. It was one of the first situation comedies, or sitcoms. In 1953, the show made history. More than 44 million people tuned in to watch the episode in which Lucy's son was born.

- *I Love Lucy* won four Emmy Awards. The Emmys started in 1949. The Academy of Television Arts & Sciences created the Emmys. The awards honor excellence in the TV industry. Emmys are awarded to different parts of the TV industry. The two most recognized Emmys are the Primetime Emmys and Daytime Emmys. The very first Emmy went to Shirley Dinsdale. It was for Outstanding Personality. Shirley was a puppeteer. She starred in the show *Judy Splinters.*

- TV has come a long way. Today you can watch TV programs on your phone and computer. Digital video recorders, or DVRs, record shows to watch later. People can catch highlights of shows on YouTube. In 2012, the Internet streaming service Netflix made TV history. It created its first TV show for its subscribers. The show was called *Lilyhammer.* In 2013, the Netflix show *House of Cards* won three Emmys. It was the first show not from a TV network to win the award.

GLOSSARY

audition
To try out for a part in a play or movie.

cinematographer
The person in charge of camera and lighting crews on a TV or film set.

comedy troupe
A group of comedians who tour and perform together.

improvisation
Performing on the spur of the moment.

producer
The person supervising a film or TV production.

sitcom
Short for situation comedy, a show in which characters share a common environment.

sketch comedy
A series of short, funny scenes.

stand-up comedy
Comedy performed in front of a live audience, in which the comedian usually speaks directly to the audience.

viral
An image or video shared widely on the Internet.

FOR MORE INFORMATION

Books

Bednar, Chuck. *Insights into American Idol.* Broomall, PA: Mason Crest, 2010.

Donovan, Sandra. *Movies and TV Top Tens.* Minneapolis, MN: Lerner Publications, 2015.

Nardo, Don. *The History of Television.* Detroit, MI: Lucent Books, 2010.

Websites

Archive of American Television
www.emmytvlegends.org

Emmy Awards
www.emmys.com

Television ratings and more
www.nielsen.com

INDEX

About the Author

Annabelle Tometich is an award-winning writer and reporter. She has written several children's books on topics ranging from lacrosse and gymnastics to nutrition and popular culture. Annabelle lives in Fort Myers, Florida, with her husband and their two really cute kids.

READ MORE FROM 12-STORY LIBRARY

Every 12-Story Library book is available in many formats, including Amazon Kindle and Apple iBooks. For more information, visit your device's store or 12StoryLibrary.com.

Run Your Own
Yard Sale

Emma Carlson Berne

PowerKiDS
press™

New York

Published in 2014 by The Rosen Publishing Group, Inc.
29 East 21st Street, New York, NY 10010

First Edition

Editor: Joanne Randolph
Book Design: Andrew Povolny
Photo Research: Katie Stryker

Photo Credits: Cover, pp. 24, 29 David Sacks/Lifesize/Thinkstock; p. 4 Joe McNally/Hulton Archive/Getty Images; p. 5 Kellie L. Folkerts/Shutterstock.com; p. 6 Ilike/Shutterstock.com; p. 7 Paul McKinnon/Shutterstock.com; p. 9 Fred Sweet/Shutterstock.com; p. 10 Romakoma/ Shutterstock.com; p. 11 Atlaspix/Shutterstock.com; p. 15 Michael C. Gray/Shutterstock. com; p. 16 Lilya Espinosa/Shutterstock.com; pp. 17, 20, 23 iStockphoto/Thinkstock; p. 18 Mat Hayward/Shutterstock.com; p. 19 Steve Debenport/E+/Getty Images; p. 22 PhotoObjects.net/Thinkstock; p. 24 Pressmaster/Shutterstock.com; p. 27 Real Deal Photo/ Shutterstock.com.

Library of Congress Cataloging-in-Publication Data

Berne, Emma Carlson.
  Run your own yard sale / by Emma Carlson Berne. — First edition.
      pages cm. — (Young entrepreneurs)
  Includes index.
  ISBN 978-1-4777-2919-9 (library) — ISBN 978-1-4777-3008-9 (pbk.) —
ISBN 978-1-4777-3079-9 (6-pack)
  1. Garage sales—Juvenile literature. 2. Young businesspeople—Juvenile literature.
  3. Entrepreneurship—Juvenile literature. I. Title.
  HF5482.3.B475 2014
  381'.195—dc23
                                          2013028071
Manufactured in the United States of America

CPSIA Compliance Information: Batch #W14PK2: For Further Information contact Rosen Publishing, New York, New York at 1-800-237-9932

Contents

Businesses Aren't Just for Adults!

Have you ever dreamed of having your own business? Maybe you thought, "Someday when I'm an adult, I can." Well, you can actually have your own business right now. You can be an **entrepreneur** at any age. An entrepreneur is a person who creates, organizes, and manages a business.

Bill Gates, shown here as a young man, is a famous entrepreneur. He started the company Microsoft with his partner Paul Allen in 1975. He is now one of the wealthiest men alive.

Not everyone will be as successful as Bill Gates, but anyone with a good business idea who is willing to work hard can be a successful entrepreneur.

To start your very own business, you will want to follow some key steps. First, you must find a need for a product or service. Then make a business plan to fulfill that need. Once you have a good plan in place, you are ready to open and run the business. If you manage your business well, you should soon start making money. For every entrepreneur, young or old, that is the best part!

How About a Yard Sale?

One of your first steps as a young entrepreneur is to look around you. Is there a need or a want in your community, at your school, or among your friends that you could fulfill? Can you think of a business that would supply your market with the need or want you identified? If there is a demand for a product or service, then that is a great start to a new business.

Have your friends help you brainstorm, or come up with some ideas for businesses. Do some research on your best ideas at the library or on the Internet.

You may see that yard sales in your neighborhood are popular. If you plan ahead, a yard sale can be a simple way to make some money.

People like to feel they are getting a good value when they buy things. For some kinds of products, buying used items can save a lot of money. In this book, you'll learn how to organize and run your own yard sale, at which you can sell used household items, clothing, and toys.

Let's Make a Plan

All good businesses have business plans. These are written documents that lay out where, when, and how you will start and run your business.

For your yard sale business plan, think about the "where" first. Will you hold your yard sale in your own yard or driveway? Perhaps you don't have a good spot on your own property. You can ask a neighbor if you can hold the sale on her lawn and then give her part of the **profits**. Maybe your church or school would let you hold the yard sale in their parking lot. Make sure that whatever spot you choose is big enough for people to move around tables of sale items easily. Think also about whether your site is a place where lots of people who might stop for your sale drive by. If your neighborhood is out of the way, you might want to think about asking to use a more public and well-traveled place for your sale.

Write your business plan down or type it on a computer. Make a list of the things you will need to get started and keep track of what you have already done.

FF 95594731 A